Journey to a New Land

AN ORAL HISTORY

BY *Kimberly Weinberger* • ILLUSTRATED BY *Tony Meers*

For information contact:
MONDO Publishing
980 Avenue of the Americas
New York, NY 10018

MONDO is a registered trademark of Mondo Publishing
Visit our web site at http://www.mondopub.com

Printed in China
00 01 02 03 04 05 06   HC   9 8 7 6 5 4 3 2 1
        02 03 04 05 06   PB   9 8 7 6 5 4 3 2
        02 03 04 05 06   BB   9 8 7 6 5 4 3 2
Designed by Jean Cohn

Library of Congress Cataloging-in-Publication Data
Weinberger, Kimberly. Journey to a new land : an oral history / by Kimberly Weinberger ; illustrated by Tony Meers.
p. cm. Summary: Elda Willitts recounts for the Ellis Island Oral History Project her childhood journey to
America from Italy in 1916. 1. Willitts, Elda Del Bino, 1909—Childhood and youth—Juvenile literature. 2. Italian-
American girls—Biography—Juvenile literature. 3. Italian Americans—Biography—Juvenile literature. 4.
Immigrants—United States—Biography—Juvenile literature. 5. Ellis Island Immigration Station (N.Y. and N.J.)—
Juvenile literature. 6. United States—Emigration and immigration—History—20th century—Juvenile literature.
7. Italy—Emigration and immigration—History—20th century—Juvenile literature. [1. Willitts, Elda Del Bino,
1909—Childhood and youth. 2. Italian Americans—Biography. 3. Immigrants. 4. Women—Biography. 5. Ellis
Island Immigration Station (N.Y. and N.J.) 6. United States—Emigration and immigration. 7. Italy—Emigration
and immigration.] I. Meers, Tony, ill. II. Title.   E 184.I8 W44 2000   973'.0451'0092—dc21   [B]   00-021810

ISBN 1-57255-811-3 (HC)   ISBN 1-57255-812-1 (pb)   ISBN 1-57255-818-0 (BB)

Introduction

Imagine leaving your home, knowing that you will never return. Imagine saying good-bye to your friends, your school, and everyone you know . . . forever. Imagine beginning a new life in a land with customs, lifestyles, and a language completely different from your own.

For many of us, such an idea seems nearly impossible. And yet, for millions of people at the turn of the twentieth century, it was a reality.

They came from all corners of Europe — countries such as Italy, Ireland, Russia, Hungary, and Poland. They came with only the clothes on their backs and their hopes for a better life. And they all came through the same gateway to freedom: Ellis Island.

For each of these immigrants who came to America there is a story. It is a story of courage and of hope, of fear and of joy. Those of us who were born in America cannot know firsthand of the struggles and hardships our ancestors faced. But we are privileged to learn from them through their oral histories — tales told by those who lived them.

Elda Del Bino Willitts was one of these immigrants. In 1916, she left her home in Italy at the age of seven. Along with her mother and six of her brothers and sisters, she boarded a steamship and set sail on the journey of a lifetime — a journey to America. This is her story.

$\mathcal{I}$ was born on April 29, 1909, in Lucca, a town in northern Italy close to the Mediterranean Sea. The youngest of eight children, I lived in a small, two-story house with my two brothers and five sisters.

Our family was very poor. It was not always easy to fill ten hungry stomachs. We lived on turnip greens and other vegetables grown in the fields around our home. Sometimes we would each dip a slice of bread in a small pot of soup and that was dinner for the night. Meat was a rare and special treat.

My parents struggled to provide for us. Papa worked long hours as a gardener for a wealthy doctor. Mama sometimes tended nearby fields to make extra money. As soon as they were able to work, the older children found jobs, too.

Then in 1912, when I was just three years old, my father made a decision that would change our lives forever. He was going to America!

Just the word "America" was enough to cause shivers of excitement in us all. The doctor Papa worked for had a home there, in a town called San Francisco. He told my father that America was a land of opportunity, a land where anything was possible. Looking at his poor and tired family, my father knew a better life was waiting there for all of us.

*E*ven with the help of the kindly doctor, Papa knew we did not have enough money for all ten of us to make the trip. He decided to take my oldest brother, Rico, with him. They would find work in America and send money to us in Italy. Once we had saved enough, the rest of us would join them. But first, we had to wait. And wait. And wait.

The passing months turned slowly into years. Without my father, life was even more difficult. To support us, four of my older sisters worked at a company making thread for clothing. Mama stayed home, cooking, cleaning, and caring for us all. Though I was young, I helped around the house as much as I could. I didn't go to school. At that time, some people in Italy didn't believe girls should be educated.

$\mathcal{F}$inally, after four years, our long wait was over — we had saved enough money for the trip! Eight passports were obtained. Eight tickets were purchased. America was waiting for us, with all the promise of a bright, new day.

$\mathcal{W}$e were scheduled to leave in the spring of 1916 on a ship called the *Ancona*. World War I was raging across Europe at that time. My brother Joe was sixteen years old — old enough to become a soldier. But, because he was going to America, Joe was told he would receive special papers that said he did not have to fight in the war.

We waited impatiently for Joe's papers to arrive. Many days passed, and still they did not come. Finally, it became too late and we had to postpone our trip. After our four-year wait, this delay seemed like a cruel joke. We all shed tears of bitter disappointment.

$\mathcal{T}$wo more weeks passed, though it felt to us like two years. Then, at last, the wonderful papers arrived. We hastily boarded a train to the Italian city of Genoa. We would now leave on a different ship, the *Caserta*.

*W*hen we reached the port of Genoa, we were greeted with shocking news: our first ship, the *Ancona*, had been torpedoed and sunk! There were no survivors.

Thinking of how near we had come to boarding that doomed ship, we decided our fate must surely be in God's hands. The delay that caused us to miss the *Ancona* proved to be the first of many blessings we would receive along our journey.

The *Caserta* set sail on April 13, 1916. We were traveling as steerage passengers, since that was the cheapest way to cross the Atlantic Ocean.

Each of us carried small bundles of blankets and what few pieces of clothing we owned. Everything else was left behind.

$\mathcal{U}$nlike first- and second-class passengers, all people traveling steerage stayed in the lower decks of the ship for the entire voyage.

The steerage section was dark, crowded and, oh, the smell! The sickening combination of unwashed people and spoiled food was bad enough. But by far, the worst odor came from the unavoidable seasickness, as the never-ending waves tossed the ship to and fro. Being the lowest-class passengers, we had very few bathrooms. Vomit sat for days on end until we could hardly breathe from the smell.

_B_ecause we were traveling during the war, the ship ran many safety drills. Remembering the _Ancona_'s fate, my heart nearly leapt out of my chest each time the drill siren sounded.

*I*t was during one of these drills early in our voyage that an officer took a liking to my sister, Eda. She was fourteen and she reminded him of his own daughter. It was lucky for us that she did! This officer arranged for our whole family to work in the kitchen or "galley" of the boat.

We spent all of our days above deck, peeling garlic and potatoes and cleaning vegetables. The officer even gave us first-class food to eat. Best of all, we were able to escape the horrors of the steerage section, even if only for the day.

Since our ship had left from Italy, nearly everyone on board spoke Italian. My family became friendly with a gentleman who had made the trip to America many times.

One day, the gentleman and I went for a walk along the deck. Looking out at the vast ocean, he said to me, "You know, when we get to Ellis Island, they're going to try to examine your eye with a hook." Horrified, I watched him point to his own eye. "Don't let them do it," he said gravely. "They did it to me and one of my eyes fell into my pocket!"

Though I could see that both of his eyes were still in his head, right where they belonged, I shuddered with fear. I vowed then and there that no hook was going to get within ten feet of me!

*H*ook or no, Ellis Island was indeed a dreaded place for all of us. If America was the land of opportunity, then Ellis Island was surely the port of fear. It was the place where our entire future would be decided.

On the ship, we heard stories of people being turned away from the island because they weren't strong or healthy enough to work. If the doctors there thought you were ill, they marked your clothing with a piece of chalk. Failing to prove you were healthy meant deportation — you would be forced to return home in disgrace, with even less than you had before you left. Many people would rather die than go back.

The voyage to America took sixteen days. My first and only memory of the morning we arrived at Ellis Island is of my family weeping. We cried with such happiness as our ship docked. After a harrowing journey, we had reached the blessed land at last. But we also cried with fear of what lay ahead. Would they let us through?

The first- and second-class passengers were examined on the ship and let off first. They did not have to face the doctors at Ellis Island. Then, finally, it was our turn.

We were led to a great hall, larger than any room I had ever seen. Inside, the room was filled wall-to-wall with people shouting, crying, waiting, and praying. Aside from a familiar Italian word here and there, I could not understand any of the countless languages being spoken all around me.

We stood in an endless line, waiting to be examined for diseases. As I got closer to the doctor, I saw a flash of shiny metal in his hand. A hook! The man from the ship was right — doctors on the island were using hooks to check people's eyes for disease.

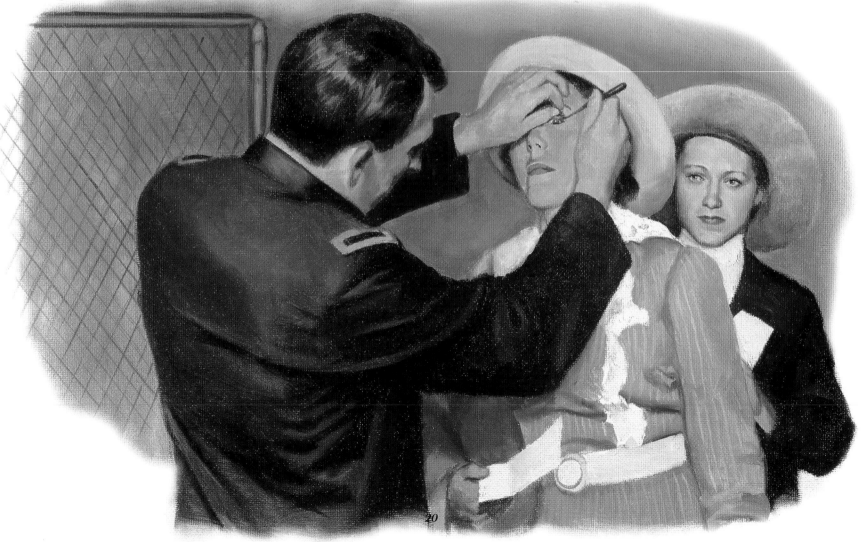

I covered my face as the doctor examined my family. Then, when it was my turn, I did what any seven-year-old child would do — I threw myself on the floor and screamed at the top of my lungs!

As the doctor scolded me, I looked up to see fear in Mama's eyes. If I did not pass the examination, we would not be allowed in America. And yet, miraculously, we were blessed once again. Seeing that my whole family had healthy eyes, the doctor let me by without an exam. We were on our way!

$\mathcal{M}$y father was working in California, a six-day train ride away. After passing through Ellis Island, we had to find the train that would bring us to our new home in San Francisco. Looking around at the strange faces and hearing this unknown language called "English," we were completely overwhelmed. Luckily, the man from the ship who had warned me about the hook was there to help us. He even traveled with us on the train as far as Chicago.

$\mathcal{M}$ama had used what was left of our money to buy boxed lunches at Ellis Island. She tried to buy enough food to last us the entire train trip.

And what strange and new food it was! Each box contained something called a "sandwich," a delicious invention we had never eaten back home. There were sweet cookies as well. To our hungry stomachs, this food was a feast. By the second day of our train trip, we had eaten every last bite. The rest of the way, we ate only candy bars — a few pieces each day to make them last.

We had to sit up the entire trip as our tickets did not allow us to ride in a sleeping car. Compared to the ship, though, the train ride was heaven.

On May 6th, we arrived in San Francisco. Papa and my brother, Rico, met us at the train and brought us to our new apartment.

As I was only three years old when he left, I could barely remember what my father looked like. Seeing him again was almost like meeting him for the first time. We all hugged and laughed and cried. But after only two days, Papa had to leave us once again to travel north for work.

𝓜y father had found a job in the town of Asti in northern California. There he worked at the Italian Swiss Colony, a place for immigrants who had come from Italy and Switzerland. Papa worked the land there and sold fruits and vegetables. He would send money and food to us in San Francisco whenever he could.

For our first few months in America, we lived in a tiny, two-bedroom apartment. With my brother Rico, we now numbered nine people. We slept three to a bed in nearly every room — even the dining room! Being the youngest, I seemed to spend half my time wedged in the middle of two sisters.

I soon began school for the first time in my life. I loved almost everything about school — the books, the teachers, even the homework. At times, though, it was difficult to fit in. Everything from the clothes I wore to the language I spoke to the food my mother made me for lunch was different. Sometimes the other children laughed at me and said mean things. I wanted more than anything to be like everyone else.

Though I suffered many embarrassing moments, I knew how truly lucky I was. Back in Italy, I might never have been given the chance to learn to read and write. But in America, anything was possible.

$\mathcal{M}$y sisters quickly found work at a nearby fruit-packing company. After three years, Papa finally came home to stay.

We moved to a bigger house, and Papa and I spent many hours together, trying to catch up on all of the lost time. I loved to help him make homemade sausages and wine. In the evenings, Papa would help me with my math homework. He was a whiz with numbers!

Papa used to love rubbing his whiskered cheek against my own. I would giggle and say, "Oh, Babbo, stop that!" And we would laugh and laugh. That was Papa's way of saying, "I love you."

The time I spent with my father proved to be even more precious than I could have known. When I was twelve years old, Papa came down with an awful case of the flu. Within three days, it had turned into pneumonia. The doctor was called, but there were no medicines at that time that could help him. On the fifth day, Papa died.

Today, looking back on the wonderful life I've led, my only regret is that Papa did not live long enough to share in my happiness. He never met my wonderful husband, Bill Willitts. He never got to hug his grandson, Bill Jr. He did not live to see the business my husband and I started here in America, or the incredible success it became.

Like millions of immigrants before and since, my parents sacrificed everything to give their children a bright future. No child could ask for a greater gift.

Ellis Island

*B*etween the years 1892 and 1954, more than 12 million men, women, and children passed through Ellis Island. They left behind them the only way of life they had ever known. For many, it was a life of poverty and suffering. Some had lived through religious persecution, others had endured the horrors of World War I and World War II. For all of them, America lay across the ocean, a beacon of hope for freedom and a better way of life.

Awaiting their arrival in New York harbor, the glorious Statue of Liberty has remained a symbol of the American dream. On her base, a poem reads:

> *Give me your tired, your poor,*
> *Your huddled masses yearning to breathe free,*
> *The wretched refuse of your teeming shore.*
> *Send these, the homeless, tempest-tost to me,*
> *I lift my lamp beside the golden door!*
>
> —EMMA LAZARUS, 1883

For millions of immigrants, that "golden door" led to a lifetime of opportunities they could only dream about in their homelands. Through their customs, languages, and memories, they enriched America with their diverse backgrounds. Through the stories they told their children and their children's children, they serve as a living history for us all.

$\mathcal{A}$s these stories are passed down from generation to generation, they often change, if only slightly, with each retelling. This, in fact, is the nature of an oral history, as each teller expands on what he or she has been told. As Elda Willitts points out, "I'm not sure if everything I've said is what I personally witnessed. My family didn't talk about much of anything else for the first few years after we came to America. Some of my memories may actually be the stories that my family shared, which became my truth as the years went on."

Standing in the massive Registry Room at Ellis Island today, it is not difficult to imagine the echoes of voices past. Walk through to the Oral History Library, and there's no need to imagine at all. Housed within the library are audio recordings of more than 1,500 interviews with immigrants from around the world — including Elda Willitts. Also available are taped conversations with doctors, nurses, and officials who worked at the island during its peak immigration years.

The Ellis Island Oral History Project began gathering these firsthand accounts in 1973. As we now enter the twenty-first century, the stories these immigrants tell remind us all of the promise America still holds — and how much we can learn from our past.